J $11.95
551.3   Wood, Jenny
Wo   Icebergs

DATE DUE

MR 2'9	AN 1 9 9		
MR 17'9	NH 1 3 9		
AP 3'9	JY 24 00		
MY 1'9	DE 12'0		
NO 6'92	SE 25 01		
AP 8'93	MY 22 02		
MY 26 9			
JY 8'93			
JUN 8 90			
AN 20 9			
JAN 14 9			
DEC 03 9			

DEMCO

WONDERWORKS OF NATURE

ICEBERGS

TITANS OF THE OCEANS

JENNY WOOD

Gareth Stevens Children's Books
MILWAUKEE

Wonderworks of Nature:

Caves: An Underground Wonderland
Icebergs: Titans of the Oceans
Storms: Nature's Fury
Volcanoes: Fire from Below

For a free color catalog describing Gareth Stevens' list of high-quality children's books, call 1-800-341-3569 (USA) or 1-800-461-9120 (Canada).

Photographic Credits: pp. 4-5 Arctic Camera; p. 6 Frank Lane Picture Agency, Ltd.; p. 7 (top) Robert Harding Picture Library, (bottom) Planet Earth Pictures; p. 8 Frank Lane Picture Agency, Ltd.; p. 9 (left inset) Frank Lane Picture Agency, Ltd., (right inset) Eric & David Hosking, (main picture) The Hutchinson Library; p. 10 The Hutchinson Library; p. 11 Robert Harding Picture Library; p. 12 Zefa; p. 13 Ardea; pp. 14-15 Eric & David Hosking; p. 16 Frank Lane Picture Agency, Ltd.; p. 17 (top) Ardea, (bottom) Survival Anglia Photo Library; p. 18 (inset) Planet Earth Pictures; pp. 18-19 Charles Swithinbank; p. 20 (top) Survival Anglia Photo Library, (bottom) Bryan and Cherry Alexander; p. 22 Survival Anglia Photo Library; p. 23 (top) Zefa, (bottom) British Antarctic Survey; cover photo (front) Tony Stone Associates, Ltd., cover photo (back) Bruce Coleman.

Illustration Credits: pp. 5, 6, 7, 11, 13, 15, 21, 22 Francis Mosley; pp. 24-28 Grahame Corbett.

Library of Congress Cataloging-in-Publication Data

Wood, Jenny.
    Icebergs: titans of the oceans / Jenny Wood. — North American ed.
        p. cm. — (Wonderworks of nature)
    Includes index.
    Summary: Text and pictures explain the formation and movement of icebergs,
as well as life on these icy masses.
    ISBN 0-8368-0470-8
    1. Icebergs—Juvenile literature. [1. Icebergs.] I. Title. II. Series: Wood, Jenny.
    Wonderworks of nature.
    GB2403.8.W66   1990
    551.3'42—dc20   90-55462

This North American edition first published in 1991 by
Gareth Stevens Children's Books
1555 North RiverCenter Drive, Suite 201
Milwaukee, Wisconsin 53212, USA

This U.S. edition copyright © 1991. First published in the United Kingdom by Two-Can Publishing, Ltd. Text copyright © 1990 by Jenny Wood.

Printed in the United States of America

1 2 3 4 5 6 7 8 9 97 96 95 94 93 92 91

CONTENTS

WHAT ARE ICEBERGS?

Icebergs are floating masses of frozen fresh water. They are found in the world's cold seas near the North and South poles. But where do they come from and how are they made?

Some of the land around the North and South poles is mountainous. Near the tops of the mountains are huge snowfields where the snow gradually turns to ice. After months, or even years, the ice becomes so heavy that it starts to move slowly downhill. These "ice rivers" are called **glaciers**. When a glacier finally reaches the sea, huge pieces of ice may break off and form floating icebergs.

Much of the Arctic, the area around the North Pole, is covered by a thick layer of ice called an **ice sheet**. Long tongues of ice extend into the sea from the edge of this ice sheet. Cracks in the ice, caused by the warmer spring weather as well as by the action of the waves, result in chunks of ice breaking off from the tongues. These too become icebergs.

An even thicker sheet of ice called the **polar ice cap** covers much of Antarctica, the area around the South Pole. Here, enormous **tabular icebergs**, so-called because of their flat, table-like tops, break off and drift out to sea.

► Icebergs drift in the cold Arctic Ocean.

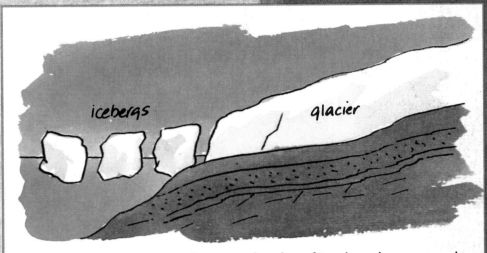

As a glacier flows into the sea, chunks of ice break away and form icebergs. Sometimes there is a terrific explosion and a noise like rolling thunder as an iceberg breaks free.

FLOATING ICE

When most things freeze, they become smaller. However, when water freezes, it expands. This means any volume of ice will always be lighter than the equal volume of liquid water. This simple fact is what makes icebergs float.

When water freezes, it forms beautiful ice crystals. The ice itself can be clear, like huge blocks of glass. However, icebergs usually look white because of tiny gas bubbles trapped in the ice or because they are covered with snow.

▶ Look at this piece of floating ice. Can you see how much of it is hidden beneath the water?

Icebergs don't float all that well. Between six-sevenths and nine-tenths of any iceberg will always be under water. The fact that so much of an iceberg is out of sight, under the sea, is what makes it such a danger to ships.

▲ Around the North and South poles, ice forms on the sea in winter.

▼ Tiny flower-like crystals form on the sea ice.

MAKE AN ICEBERG

You can see for yourself how ice floats by filling a glass with water and dropping in two ice cubes. When you have finished watching your icebergs, you can drink your experiment!

ICEBERG SHAPES AND SIZES

Icebergs come in all shapes and sizes. The largest icebergs can rise more than 400 feet (120 meters) above the sea, and the tabular bergs may be many miles (kilometers) long. Some icebergs look like mountains. Others have been compared to towers, church spires, pyramids, cathedrals, and palaces. Many are molded into unusual and fascinating shapes by the action of the wind and the waves. The process of melting causes an iceberg to change shape, too.

DID YOU KNOW?

● The largest iceberg ever recorded was 208 miles (335 km) long and 60 miles (97 km) wide, a total of 12,000 square miles (31,000 km^2) – larger than Belgium!

● The tallest iceberg ever recorded was 550 feet (167 m) high – just over half the height of the Eiffel Tower in Paris!

ICE ON THE MOVE

Icebergs are formed in the two coldest regions of the world, the Arctic and the Antarctic.

Arctic icebergs come mainly from Greenland. This huge island is almost entirely covered by an ice sheet. The icebergs break off, float down the coast and out into the Atlantic Ocean. In May, June, and July they drift down the eastern coast of North America. Ocean liners traveling between Europe and New York always follow a more southerly route during these early summer months to avoid the drifting bergs.

Ships and airplanes report the position of icebergs to the International Ice Patrol, which keeps track of the movement of icebergs in the Atlantic and estimates the routes they might take.

▼ A group of Antarctic icebergs float in open water during the summer season. Icebergs can travel up to 16 miles (25 km) per day.

▲ A tabular berg drifts away from an ice shelf into warmer waters.

The weather in the Antarctic is much colder and stormier than in the Arctic, and southern icebergs tend to be much bigger than northern ones. Most are tabular bergs which break off from the massive **ice shelves** that make up 30 percent of Antarctica's coastline.

It can take years for an iceberg to melt. Although the wind and sun melt its surface as it drifts along on the ocean currents, the bottom section, which is under water, melts much more slowly. But when an iceberg reaches warmer waters, the melting process speeds up and the berg begins to break up into hundreds of small pieces. Eventually these melt completely and disappear.

DID YOU KNOW?

● An Arctic iceberg has reached as far south as the island of Bermuda, a journey of 2,500 miles (4,000 km), and an Antarctic iceberg has reached almost as far north as Rio de Janeiro, a journey of 3,440 miles (5,500 km).

LIVING ON ICEBERGS

The icy seas and land masses of the Arctic and the Antarctic may seem unlikely places for animals to live, but they are home to certain types of penguins, seals, and whales as well as to walruses and polar bears. Each of these animals is specially adapted for living there. A penguin, for example, has short, tightly packed feathers which form a waterproof covering over its body as well as a layer of fat under its skin to keep it warm in the cold water. Some seals have a layer of fat, too. Others have thick fur to protect them against the cold.

Walruses

Walruses are members of the seal family and are found in the Arctic, near the North Pole. They live in groups called colonies, and often drift along lying on icebergs. An adult male can reach up to 12 feet (3.7 m) in length and can weigh up to 3,080 pounds (1,400 kilograms).

The walrus spends much of its time in the water, digging for food on the seabed with its long tusks. Clams, mussels, and shrimps are its favorite meal. It crushes the shells in its mouth then spits them out, swallowing only the soft, fleshy parts of the fish. The moustache of long stiff whiskers on the walrus' face helps guide the food into its mouth.

▲ A walrus' tusks are long, upper teeth. Sometimes a walrus digs its tusks into the ice as support while it hauls itself out of the water.

▶ A humpback whale is a baleen whale. It eats krill and grows up to 50 feet (15 m) long.

Whales

All whales live in the sea. Most are toothed whales, which feed on fish and animals such as seals. They have short cone-shaped teeth. But others are **baleen** whales, which feed on tiny shrimp-like creatures called **krill**. Instead of teeth, a baleen whale has a series of bony plates hanging from the roof of its mouth. These act like a sieve and help the whale catch the tiny krill.

Toothed whales are constantly on the move around the world's oceans, following the shoals of fish they feed on. Baleen whales, on the other hand, make regular journeys between summer feeding grounds and winter breeding areas.

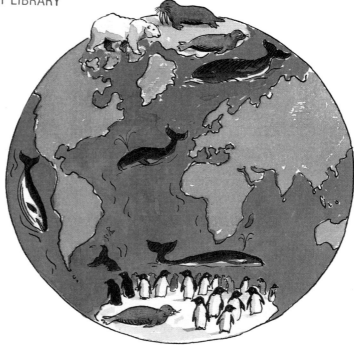

▲ Polar bears and walruses live only in the Arctic, penguins only in the Antarctic. Seals are found in both places, and whales swim in most of the world's seas.

Polar bears

The polar bear is one of the largest and most ferocious land-living carnivores (meat-eaters). Polar bears are found over an area of 12 million square miles (31 million km^2) of Arctic ice.

In winter all polar bears head south toward Greenland in search of food. By trotting over the ice and swimming through the icy sea, they can travel up to 40 miles (64 km) in a day.

They mainly eat seals, although they have learned to scavenge from rubbish dumps and even houses in the towns of northern Canada.

Polar bears are superbly adapted for the cold. Their bodies are covered with a layer of fat called **blubber** and thick fur.

Pregnant female polar bears dig large dens in snowdrifts at the start of winter. The tunnel to the outside always slopes downward, trapping the warm air in the den. In December the cubs are born. They are blind and completely helpless. They feed off their mother's rich milk. In March, they go out on the ice for the first time.

Penguins

Adelie penguins are one of the seven species of penguin that live in the Antarctic region. They spend most of each year at sea, but return to land to lay their eggs and raise their chicks. Once a year, too, they come ashore to **molt**. Their old feathers fall out and are replaced by new ones growing underneath.

Penguins cannot fly, but their paddle-shaped wings, short legs, and webbed feet are perfectly designed for life in the water. Moving on land is more difficult. They must either waddle slowly or fall forward on their chests and toboggan across the ice.

DID YOU KNOW?

● At the end of summer, each female Emperor penguin lays one egg, then returns to the ocean. The male keeps the egg warm all winter in a fold of skin on top of his feet. He eats nothing and by the time the female returns he has lost 40 percent of his body weight.

◀ These Adelie penguins are diving into the water in search of fish. They have special spikes inside their mouths to help them hold on to their slippery prey. They can store the food inside their bodies, in special pouches called crops.

▼ A baby seal is called a pup. It is left to survive on its own when it is about six weeks old.

▲ Three harbor seals rest on Arctic ice. Seals cannot remain beneath the surface continuously for more than twenty minutes.

Seals

Like penguins, seals are ideally suited for living in the water. Their smooth, streamlined bodies, **flippers**, and short, strong tails make them excellent swimmers. On land they move slowly, wriggling and sliding across the ice.

Seals spend most of their lives at sea, but come ashore to mate and give birth to their young.

At one time, seals were killed for their fur which was used to make coats, hats, and boots. Now many people do not like wearing clothes made of animal fur, and the killing of seals in large numbers is forbidden.

ICEBREAKERS

An icebreaker is a ship which has been designed to travel through ice-covered waters. It has a specially shaped **bow** and a reinforced **hull**. Icebreakers move slowly but steadily, pushing their bows up on top of the ice until the weight of the ship causes the ice to collapse. The largest icebreakers are designed to break ice that is 8 feet (2.4 m) thick. But by reversing and then ramming the ice, some can actually break through ice more than 23 feet (7 m) thick!

Icebreakers are used to rescue ships trapped in ice, conduct scientific research, and escort supply ships. The Soviet Union uses some of the world's largest icebreakers to clear ice from its shipping lanes in the Arctic.

▲ A pause in the journey while some research is carried out on the ice.

CROSSING THE ICE

In the past, explorers crossed the ice on foot or used sleds pulled by **huskies**. Modern explorers can choose from many different means of transportation.

The fastest way of traveling across the ice is by air. Large planes are fitted with skis so they can land on the snow. Helicopters can land on single icebergs. Tractors called snowcats, with caterpillar tracks, carry heavy loads across the ice. Lightweight snow scooters, known as skidoos, skim quickly over the surface.

▼ Huskies have pulled sleds across the ice for hundreds of years.

▲ Tents must be securely pitched, as strong winds and blizzards can occur quite suddenly.

THE *TITANIC*

On the night of April 14, 1912, the passenger liner RMS *Titanic* was steaming through the North Atlantic. She was the biggest ship ever built and this was her first voyage. The 2,227 passengers and crew were enjoying themselves, secure in the knowledge that the ship was unsinkable.

Just before midnight, some of the passengers felt a slight jolt and wondered what it was. They did not know that the great liner had hit an iceberg, nor did they realize that within two hours the *Titanic* would sink to the bottom of the ocean.

The "unsinkable" ship only had enough lifeboats for half the people aboard. In fact only 705 were actually rescued. The remaining passengers and crew were either carried to the bottom of the sea as the huge liner made its final plunge, or frozen to death in the icy water.

▼ The end of the *Titanic*.

WORKING ON THE ICE

A lot of people work on the ice. The Arctic, for example, is an important oil-producing area. Oil rigs drill for oil which is then pumped southward along a pipeline over 750 miles (1,200 km) long.

There are also several scientific stations in the polar regions. Scientists study the animals and other wildlife. They have found that many animals are in danger of extinction because of over-fishing and **pollution**.

Chemicals used in aerosol sprays have damaged the Antarctic ozone layer which protects us from the sun's dangerous ultraviolet radiation. A similar hole has now been found over the Arctic.

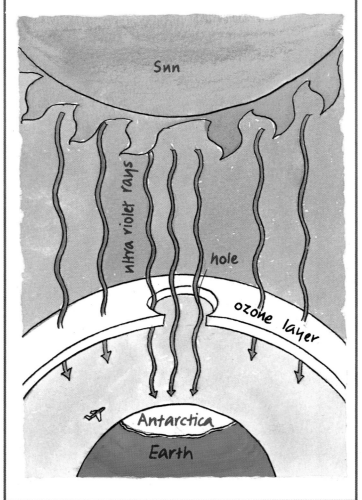

◄ A scientist explores the underwater world below the Antarctic ice. Biologists are fascinated by the variety of life forms which exist in these icy waters.

► The Faraday Scientific Station is on the west coast of the Antarctic peninsula. It is a laboratory for studying the atmosphere.

Scientists who study the weather have discovered that earth's atmosphere is starting to warm up as a result of the **greenhouse effect**. They have also found evidence of serious pollution. One of their most recent discoveries is a huge hole that has appeared in the **ozone layer** of the atmosphere over Antarctica. This will allow more **ultraviolet radiation** from the sun to reach the earth. These ultraviolet rays will cause an increase in skin cancer. Reports of the ozone hole have alarmed people all over the world. But it may be too late to repair the damage.

▲ In 1968, oil was discovered in Prudhoe Bay, which lies in Alaska's Arctic Coastal Plain. Oil is now Alaska's most valuable mineral product.

THE STORY OF THREE WHALES

On the morning of October 7, 1988, Roy Ashmaogak left his home in the small town of Barrow, in the northwest of Alaska, to hunt for seals. The weather was bitterly cold. Winter had come early, and the sea around Barrow had already frozen over. But Roy had lived in Barrow all his life, so he was used to the freezing temperatures and to being surrounded by ice and snow for months on end. He had hunted seals in conditions like these many times.

But this was no ordinary day. As Roy tramped across the ice, something caught his eye. As he moved closer, he saw an extraordinary sight. Three California gray whales were pushing their great heads through a crack in the ice! They seemed anxious and frightened. Roy realized at once that the whales were trapped. There was ice everywhere. The whales' noses were scraped and bruised from trying to force a way through to the open sea.

Roy guessed that the three whales must have been left behind when the rest of their herd began the long swim south from their summer feeding grounds in the Arctic Ocean to their winter breeding grounds in the warm waters of California. Surprised by the sudden, early arrival of winter they seemed to have lost their sense of direction. Instead of heading for open water, they had swum into a shallow bay where the water had quickly frozen over and formed a wall of ice at the bay's mouth. There was no way out.

Whales need to come up to the surface about every four minutes to breathe. Roy knew that something had to be done soon to help the whales. They had managed to make one small breathing hole, but the ice was thick and they were too weak to create any more. Roy raced back to Barrow to look for help.

Everyone listened to Roy's story, but at first nothing was done. Many people felt that, sad though it was, the whales should be left to die. But others began to feel differently. A woman called Cindy Lowry began to try to interest people in the idea of saving the whales. Soon the story of the whales appeared in local newspapers and on television. The Inuit people of Barrow trooped out on to the ice with chainsaws and pickaxes to try to cut more breathing holes for the whales and guide them through to open water.

Before long, people all round the world had heard about the three whales. Scientists and others who wanted to help began to flock to Barrow to see what could be done. Even Ronald Reagan, the president of the United States at the time, offered his help.

But was it too late? By now, the Inuit had worked for fourteen days and nights to cut a line of breathing holes in the ice, leading toward the sea. But the holes kept freezing over and, in any case, the whales seemed too frightened to follow the trail. To make matters worse, the youngest whale, nicknamed Bone, was ill. It was wheezing with pneumonia and trying to rest its battered head on the ice shelf. Sadly, on Friday, October 21, it died.

The two older whales, nicknamed Crossbeak and Bonnet, were tiring. Something had to be done quickly if they were to escape from their ice prison. An enormous ice barge, which looked like a gigantic bulldozer, tried to smash a path through the ice, but it got stuck. Then a sky-crane helicopter hammered the ice with a concrete weight. It punched a line of holes from the whales to the ice wall at the mouth of the bay, but Crossbeak and Bonnet still would not move. It seemed that they too would die. The rescuers were frantic. They were beginning to think they might have to try to airlift the whales to safety in a huge net slung from a helicopter! But they were worried about this idea. It had never been tried before and a California gray whale, although not the largest type of whale by any means, still weighs about 66,000 pounds (30,000 kilograms)!

Then, on the twentieth day, Wednesday, October 26, just as everyone had almost given up hope, a Russian icebreaker roared to the rescue. All day and all night the huge ship charged at the ice, smashing it into tiny pieces. By the morning of the following day, part of the ice wall at the bay's mouth had been destroyed and a clear, narrow channel led from the whales to the open sea. A great cheer went up from the captain and his crew and from all the others who had been involved in the rescue. Three weeks after they had first been spotted, the whales were free!

The icebreaker turned and headed homeward. The whales followed close behind. At last they were on their way to join the rest of the herd on the long journey south.

TRUE OR FALSE?

Which of these facts are true and which ones are false?
If you have read this book carefully, you will know the answers.

1 A glacier is a type of iceberg.

2 Antarctic icebergs tend to be bigger than those found in the Arctic.

3 Between one-seventh and one-tenth of an iceberg is under water.

4 Walruses are found in the Arctic.

5 Tiny gas bubbles trapped in the ice cause an iceberg to look white.

6 The International Ice Patrol monitors the movement of icebergs in Antarctica.

7 Killer whales are baleen whales.

8 Female polar bears give birth to their cubs in snow dens which they dig at the start of winter.

9 The largest iceberg ever recorded was the same size as Belgium.

10 Icebergs are often molded into unusual shapes by the action of the wind and the waves.

11 There are two main groups of icebergs – tabular and rounded.

12 An icebreaker is a type of sled used for traveling across the ice.

13 Penguins cannot fly.

Answers: 1 False: 2 True: 3 False: 4 True: 5 True: 6 False: 7 False: 8 True: 9 False: 10 True: 11 False: 12 False: 13 True.

GLOSSARY

Baleen is a horn-like material made of keratin, the same substance as hair and nails. Instead of teeth, some types of whales have a series of baleen plates in their mouth.

Blubber is a layer of fat under the skin. Many animals who live in cold areas of the world have blubber to help keep them warm.

Bow is the name given to the front or "fore-end" of a boat or ship.

Flippers are limbs used by animals such as seals who spend all or most of their lives in water, to help them swim well.

Glacier is the name given to a slowly moving river of ice.

Greenhouse effect is the phrase used to describe the warming of the earth caused by gases which have been released into the atmosphere. Nobody is quite sure what the final effect will be, but if the earth continues to warm up, the ice at the poles will begin to melt. This will make the sea levels rise and eventually a lot of land could disappear underwater.

Hull is the name given to the body or frame of a ship.

Huskies are dogs used in the Arctic for pulling sleds across the ice.

Ice sheet is a thick layer of ice which extends over a vast area.

Ice shelf is a great ledge of ice which projects from the edge of an ice sheet.

Irregular iceberg is the name used to describe an iceberg which does not have a regular shape.

Krill are small, shrimp-like creatures. In the summer, they are found in huge swarms in the seas around Antarctica. They are eaten by baleen whales.

Molt means to lose feathers or hair. Once a year, many animals and birds molt. Their old feathers or hair fall out, to be replaced by new growth underneath.

Ozone layer is the name given to the layer of earth's atmosphere which protects us from the dangerous effects of the sun's ultraviolet rays.

Polar icecap is the name of the ice sheet which covers most of Antarctica.

Pollution "Pollute" means "to make something dirty." Human beings are making the earth "dirty" by introducing harmful substances into the environment.

Rounded iceberg is the name used to describe an iceberg whose shape has been "rounded" and softened by the effects of the wind and the waves.

Tabular iceberg is the name used to describe huge, flat icebergs with table-like tops.

Ultraviolet radiation is the harmful effect caused by the sun's ultraviolet rays. Ultraviolet is the part of the sunlight which causes a suntan, but it also causes skin cancer. These problems will increase if the ozone layer is damaged any further and is no longer able to protect us from the ultraviolet rays.

INDEX